The stately, unfashionably dressed figure at Bicentennial Plaza, posing above colorful marigolds in summer, is the symbolic first citizen of North Carolina and inspiration for the name of the capital city, Sir Walter Raleigh. Although Raleigh did not personally explore or settle land that became North Carolina, and certainly knew nothing of the Piedmont region of the state, he planned and secured funds and the ship for the first "Citie of Raleigh" (note English spelling) on Roanoke Island.

On Union Square, the block on which the Capitol building stands, three uniformed figures mark the tragic decade of 1965-1975. Two are alert, wary, supporting their wounded comrade. The North Carolina Vietnam Veterans Memorial, dedicated on Memorial Day weekend in 1987 was a project of the state's Memorial Committee begun in 1982, the same year of the completion of the national Vietnam monument, "the Wall," in Washington, D.C.

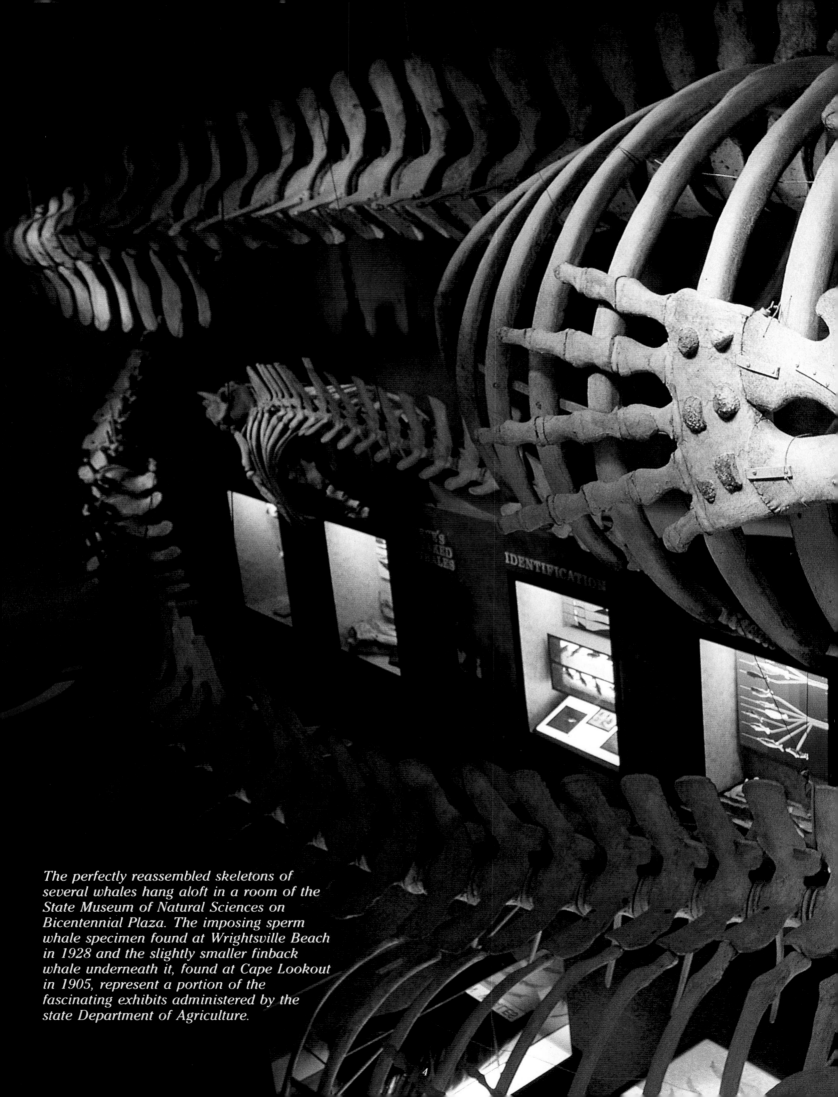

The perfectly reassembled skeletons of several whales hang aloft in a room of the State Museum of Natural Sciences on Bicentennial Plaza. The imposing sperm whale specimen found at Wrightsville Beach in 1928 and the slightly smaller finback whale underneath it, found at Cape Lookout in 1905, represent a portion of the fascinating exhibits administered by the state Department of Agriculture.

FROM
EEP

DOLPHINS

5

An exquisite sunset provides the backdrop for the hub of North Carolina recreation each October, the State Fair in Raleigh.

From first light to color-packed sundown, Jordan Lake west of Apex draws boaters, fishermen, and other pleasure-seekers from Raleigh and surrounding towns. Some 14,000 or so acres of water can shelter lots of largemouth bass, bluegill and crappie, but c'mon, you can find them.

The final formal ceremony for young women at Peace College, graduation, is the culmination of two years of study and development in a Christian environment in one of the oldest colleges in Raleigh. Perhaps with no intent to symbolize their school's name, but with a sensitivity to both inner and outward beauty and serenity the graduates dressed in white encircle the fountain in front of Main Building. In a traditional gesture, each girl tosses one of her dozen red roses into the water to symbolize that she leaves a small part of herself behind.

Library of Congress Catalogue Number: 88-71898

Hardcover ISBN: 0-917631-06-4

Printed in Spain by Cayfosa, Barcelona, through Four Colour Imports, Louisville, Kentucky.

Produced and distributed by Lightworks, 6005 Chapel Hill Road, Raleigh, N.C. 27607. Telephone (919) 851-0518 or (800) 334-3296 in North Carolina.

RALEIGH
FOR THE PEOPLE

Text and captions by Jane Collins

Photography by Raleigh Photographers Chip Henderson, Steve Muir,
Steve Murray, Michael O'Brien, Carol Fantelli, Scott Larson,
and Simon Griffiths

Design by Russell Avery, Avery Designs

Published by Capitol Broadcasting Company, Inc.

Black-and-white photographs were supplied by North Carolina State Division of
Archives and History. Photograph of Itzhak Perlman was used by permission of
Friends of the College and two photographs of the NCSU Engineering School were
supplied by the School.

Joseph Gales (1761-1841) was an English newspaperman and reformer who edited the Raleigh Register *from his first year in Raleigh, 1799, until his retirement in 1833. When the statehouse burned in 1831, Gales was serving the city as mayor. He is credited by some with having proposed the first railroad for the purpose of transporting inexpensive, durable stone for the rebuilding of the statehouse and the preservation of Raleigh as the capital of North Carolina. Gales' two sons and son-in-law also took turns as* Register *editors.*

A BEGINNING[1]

The sprawling capital of North Carolina stretches in every direction from its historic focal point at Union Square and the Capitol. It splashes beyond the semi-circular beltline in genial neighborhoods and wooded office parks, with north as its goal. It is the seat of authority for the state, comfortable in friendly surroundings. The present government buildings in Raleigh, built beginning in the late nineteenth century to replace older private structures about Union Square, are dignified, utilitarian structures, but anyone seeking information regarding specific offices within is likely to receive it from a courteous, helpful man or woman ambling by. Bureaucratic needs have widened the governmental center by a few blocks, but the State of North Carolina essentially is administered from its original geographic base.

Raleigh was not the unanimous choice for its seat of government. In fact, it did not exist when Edenton on Albemarle Sound served as capital of the colony from 1722 until 1743, nor when New Bern succeeded Edenton as capital of the colony and then of the state between 1746 and 1792. The selection of Raleigh by the North Carolina General Assembly, which had been meeting in various capital-minded towns each year, is largely attributed to its central east-west location in the state. It was hoped, too, that the Neuse River could be made navigable so that the permanent seat of government would have access to a commerical waterway. In the first quarter of the nineteenth century there were attempts made to open the Neuse from Smithfield to the mouth of Crabtree Creek in Wake County, but these proved unfeasible.

In Raleigh's first year as a town, 1792, the area incorporated was 400 acres. This portion came from a 1,000-acre tract freshly purchased from Joel Lane. Lane, like many plantation owners during colonial and post-Revolutionary days, added an inn or tavern or "ordinary" as some were called, near a public road through his estate, to provide food and lodging for overnight travelers and their horses. Some such establishments were actually in the homes of citizens licensed to operate them. Lane's property was west of, but not far from, the 400 acres that were plotted as Raleigh. As a Justice of the Peace appointed for Wake County by Colonial Governor Tryon, and as a member of the "Inferior Court of Pleas and Quarter Sessions" for the new county of Wake, Lane was a notable citizen. It is thought that the first court session was held at his home, and it was at an adjacent site that Wake's first courthouse was erected. *continued*

---

[1]In researching the early history and development of Raleigh, I made use of all hard-bound volumes available that dealt with the general subject, several publications published by the State Department of Archives and History, and some related materials. I am particularly appreciative of the comprehensive history. *WAKE: Capital County of North Carolina,* Volume I, by Elizabeth Reid Murray, and of Mrs. Murray's help in editing this text.

The North Carolina Institution for the Education of the Deaf, Dumb, and Blind has had several locations and functions since its opening in 1845. Two of its organizers were Dr. William McPheeters, pastor of the Presbyterian Church, and Joseph Gales, editor of the Raleigh Register. *Techniques for teaching deaf children were presented to the state legislators and had the support of Governor John Motley Morehead. This view is from the corner of Jones and Dawson streets on Caswell Square. Notice the early street light overhead.*

Until sometime after 1900, when it was demolished for land use, the Devereux House, or "Will's Forest," on the northwest outskirts of town, was an important center for the elite of Raleigh. The imposing example of Greek revival architecture draws together familiar names in Raleigh history: it was built by Nancy Lane Mordecai's daughter, Margaret, and her husband, Confederate Major John Devereux.

Lane was the only Wake Countian immortalized by having one of the first Raleigh streets named for him. In the basic plan, the state's eight court districts were used for names of streets: New Bern, Edenton, Morgan, Salisbury, Halifax, Wilmington, Fayetteville, and Hillsborough. Nine streets were named for the commissioners who selected Lane's property: Hargett, Dawson, McDowell, Martin, Blount, Jones, Bloodworth, Harrington, and Person. The remaining four streets honored Senate Speaker William Lenoir, House Speaker Stephen Cabarrus, Revolutionary General William R. Davis, and Joel Lane.

These twenty-one streets, bounded by the logically-named ones, North, South, East, and West, separated the 400 acres into 254 one-acre lots. Most of the lots were sold and the proceeds used to build the first Capitol, known as the statehouse. Union Square, largest of the plots and reserved for the site of the statehouse, lay centrally from east to west, but not exactly in the middle from north to south. Four other four-acre squares were kept as parks equidistant from Union Square. Clockwise from the northwest, they are Caswell Square, on which the first State School for the Deaf and Blind was later built; Burke Square, which was used as land for Raleigh Academy as early as 1804 but which became the site of the Governor's Mansion in 1891; Moore Square, for several decades the site of both schools and church buildings; and Nash Square, where the Gum Spring School was located from the late 1850s until after the Civil War. For most years Moore and Nash have been city parks.

On Union Square North Carolina's first government building was erected on land partially cleared of young hickory and oak trees. It was a less-than-elegant structure, two stories of brick on a stone foundation, and not considered attractive by some whose reactions have been recorded and preserved. Large numbers of workmen, black and white, utilized "brick yards" that had been established nearby. Slave and free, they labored at brickmaking, masonry, plastering, and carpentry, taking most of 1793 and 1794 for the task. Remodeled in 1821-22 to receive Canova's celebrated statue of George Washington, and improvements made soon after, it remained the young state's only central office another decade before it was accidentally destroyed by fire in 1831. It was then replaced by the Capitol that has served the state since 1840.

North Carolina's chief officer, the governor, was required early on to spend six months of the year in Raleigh, and later, full time, during his term in office. Although Burke Square was suggested as a suitable location for a governor's home in the early designation of lots, such a home was not built immediately. One of Raleigh's earliest two-story residences was purchased for the governor at the southwest corner of

continued

As though viewing Raleigh from a balloon aloft, an artist sketched the city as it was in 1872, including the Capitol, Christ Church, the Presbyterian Church, Metropolitan Hall, Wake County Courthouse and Jail, Yarborough House, Shaw Collegiate Institute, the old fairgrounds, Governor Charles Manly's estate, and the North Carolina Railroad tracks.

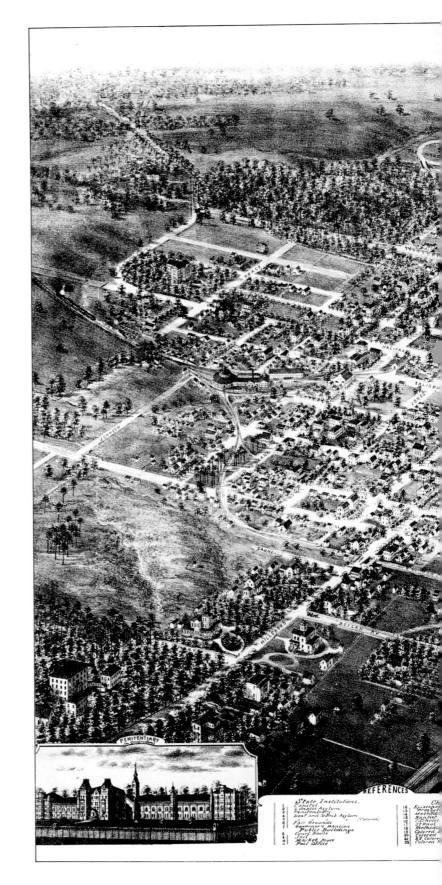

BIRD'S EYE VIEW OF THE CITY OF

RALEIGH

NORTH CAROLINA

1872

REFERENCES

Miscellaneous
23 St Mary's College
24 Peace Institute
25 Baptist School
26 Raleigh Male Academy
28 Shaw Collegiate Institute
29 St Augustine School
30 Colored Methodist School
31 United States Barracks
32 Rail Road Depot
33 City Cemetery
34 New Cemetery
    Confederate Cemetery

35 U S Cemetery
36 Tucker's Hall
37 Masonic Hall
    Manufacturing Establishments
38 Gas Works
39 Raleigh & Gaston R.R.S Machine Shops
40 N C Agricultural Machine Works
41 Adams & Sons Foundry
42 Blind & Sash Factory
43 Saw Mill
    Hotels
45 National Hotel
46 Yarborough House
47 City Hotel

LUNATIC ASYLUM
REAR VIEW

The Yarborough House, complete with additions to each end of the original building, looked like this 1885-or-so drawing approximately 35 years into its successful life of three-quarters of a century. In its viable location opposite the Wake County Courthouse on Fayetteville Street, the Yarborough boasted separate accommodations for ladies with their own entrance and social rooms, bathing rooms in the basement of the north wing, and splendid meals. A Thanksgiving Day menu of the era reads: "Oysters, Lobsters, Consomme Imperial, Sheepshead Hollandaise, Potatoes a la Maitre, Roast Sirloin, Lamb with Mint, Stuffed Turkey, Roast Canvasback Duck, Plum Pudding with Brandy Sauce," vegetables, desserts, and a variety of alcoholic beverages. The hotel survived well into the twentieth century when in 1928, on Independence Day eve, it was destroyed by fire. The city watched the uncontrollable flames and mourned.

On Morgan Street at the Capitol grounds, about 1875 and a decade after the conclusion of the Civil War, the Raleigh Light Infantry, in the company of onlookers, stands in review.

Fayetteville and Hargett streets. Several used it, but at least two governors preferred to rent their own quarters. The second home of the governor was a large brick "palace" at the foot of Fayetteville Street, constructed in 1816. At the "palace," or Government House in 1825, Governor Hutchins G. Burton entertained a particularly revered guest, General Marquis de Lafayette, French champion of the American Revolutionary War. In 1865, at the close of another war, the Governor's "palace" was occupied by Union General William T. Sherman. Afterward, it was never again used by a governor. In the quarter-century that passed before the state again provided its governors with an executive residence, they lived either in their own Raleigh homes or in rented rooms in hotels. During that period and for all of its 75 years, the Yarborough House was Raleigh's finest and most prominent hotel.

The Governor's Mansion on Burke Square was first occupied in 1891. In design it employs a combination of Queen Anne, an adaptation of a popular eighteenth-century architectural style, and Eastlake, a Victorian sub-style. The reaction of citizens and visitors to the Governor's Mansion must have differed from that referring to the statehouse a century earlier. President Franklin D. Roosevelt has been quoted as saying that the executive mansion in North Carolina was the most beautiful in the nation.

Historic Raleigh has been preserved in some fashion, but much was tragically lost by fire or replaced by something deemed an improvement. One scene can be re-created with some authenticity: From the south side of the statehouse, one looked toward Fayetteville Street. It was here that Peter Casso had an inn, or tavern, at the corner of Morgan and Fayetteville streets where the Justice Building stands now. Casso's was a very early social center where the stage stopped, horses were cared for, grain-houses and smokehouses and a "good garden" were the source of meals, and the legislators could meet. In the yard a cockpit was a scene of raucous, high-stakes gambling. On Casso's property was the humble dwelling of employees Jacob and Mary Johnson. The Johnsons were the parents of two sons; one, Andrew, born in 1808, became president of the United States following the assassination of his predecessor, Abraham Lincoln. Young Andrew lived in Raleigh only until he was sixteen, but for some years he must have looked daily at his state's capitol across Morgan Street, never suspecting that he would one day occupy the nation's capitol as its commander-in-chief.

From the first, Raleigh was a city of churches. Christ Church Parish was organized in 1821; its present building, erected between 1848 and 1853, replaced its first (1829) structure at the same location, *continued*

Fayetteville Street, shown here as recently as 1909, featured banks, businesses, and hotels, and an expedient way to get to all of them: the trolley. The building in the center of the photograph, with the conspicuous spire is Metropolitan Hall built in 1870 to house a public auditorium, city offices, a public market, and quarters for fire and police offices.

A Salisbury Street building was one of Raleigh's early fire stations. This scene has been identified as Raleigh's "Championship" Volunteer Rescue Steam Fire Engine Company, one of its many fire-fighting championships in statewide competitions.

Wilmington Street between New Bern Avenue and Edenton Street. Its architecture is Gothic Revival, characterized by pointed arches, stained glass, spires, and steep gabled roofs. Christ Church is made of local granite and has a freestanding tower.

Bishop John Stark Ravenscroft was the church's first rector; Dr. George W. Freeman filled the office in the 1830s. From 1840 until his death the rector was Richard Sharpe Mason. Mason was one of the incorporators of St. Augustine's College and an outspoken supporter of improved farming methods.

Mason's wife, Mary Ann Mason, was the first native North Carolinian to publish a book for children. *A Wreath from the Woods of Carolina* presented ten moralistic stories supporting good behavior and was illustrated with colored engravings of her own sketches of native wild flowers. During this period she also wrote another book, although it was not immediately published. The *Young Housewife's Counsellor and Friend* included a variety of subjects. Mrs. Mason's cameos and plaster medallions, another avenue of her talent, were obviously the work of a skillful artist.

On another side of Union Square, at the corner of Edenton and Salisbury streets, First Baptist Church was dedicated in 1858. It, too, is an example of Gothic architecture, more accurately, neo-Gothic, and is very different from Christ Church. First Baptist is made of stuccoed walls and is raised on a high podium built close to the street. Two examples of churches whose building locations date back to Raleigh's early years, but whose facilities have replaced their earlier buildings, are First Presbyterian, whose original structure was the first brick church building in Raleigh in 1818; and First Baptist Church on Wilmington Street, a twentieth-century successor to an earlier church.

Through the years, the deliberately-plotted streets of Raleigh have supported construction of varied types to bring to the state capital and growing county seat the necessities and conveniences of government, education, business, health, communication, transportation, and spiritual and cultural enrichment. Along with the statehouse, county courthouse and eventually the municipal offices, Raleigh devised and developed both private and public schools. Six colleges emerged in the half-century between 1842 and 1899 which continue to operate: The first was St. Mary's, an Episcopal school for girls. No straw bonnets, lace, artificial flowers, nor jewelry were permitted, but the school was so successful that it remained open during the Civil War. Peace, a Presbyterian college also for women, was chartered in 1857, and its building served as a military hospital before it opened as a college. In 1879, Peace Institute had the first kindergarten in the South. Shaw University was begun by Dr. Henry Martin Tupper, a former Union

continued

Raleigh, N. C. Baptist University for Women.

Meredith College, a 225-acre Christian school of liberal arts for women, came into existence as Baptist Female University in a downtown location, at the corner of Blount and Edenton streets. Main building, represented here, was at first the entire school, and contained lodgings, classrooms, laboratories, chapel, dining room, and library. Chartered and founded in 1891, it was not until 1899 that the school was ready to receive its first students. In 1909, the college was renamed in honor of its founder, Thomas Meredith, editor of Raleigh's Biblical Recorder. *When the campus was moved to Hillsborough Street in 1926, Main became the Mansion Park Hotel. It was razed in 1967.*

In attire that is somewhat more updated than that shown in the previous scene, young women of Meredith College opt for improvisation before the camera. While the Christian perspective continues to be emphasized, the college also continues to provide women with excellent educational opportunities. These students might not have expected to find the curricula available in the 1980s, including masters degree programs in business administration, education, and music.

Army private and chaplain. With an emphasis on theology, this institution provided the nation's first black medical school in 1881, and in 1874 constructed Estey Hall, the first college building erected in America solely for the education of black women. St. Augustine's College in 1867 had two aims: to educate black teachers and to prepare blacks for Episcopal ministry. Its subsequent history has brought it into full, four-year accreditation with approximately 1,700 students enrolled from thirty-two states and twenty foreign countries, tackling the major course studies of computer science, engineering, pre-law, pre-med, and communications. North Carolina College of Agriculture and Mechanical Arts, now North Carolina State University, began in 1889 as one of the nation's land-grant institutions and has become a major state university. Finally, Meredith College was chartered in 1891 and opened in 1899 as the Baptist Female University. In 1926 it moved away from the Capitol area to its present location on Hillsborough Street.

As shops and businesses opened on Fayetteville Street and New Bern Avenue, banks and savings institutions opened offices and branches alongside of them. The first two were Raleigh branches of the Bank of Cape Fear and of the Bank of New Bern, followed by the State Bank of North Carolina. The 1814 headquarters for the last-named survives on New Bern Avenue and is considered the oldest brick building in Wake County. Some of the earliest services were clock and watch repair, a bakery, two saddle shops, a general merchandise store, and a federal post office. By 1800, when the town was only eight years old, three book stores were flourishing. By 1820, carpentry and blacksmithing were popular trades in and around Raleigh and within Wake County, agriculture remained, as it had always been, the primary occupation. The little city kept pace with goods and services to complement the agricultural strides of the rural farmers.

In a span of about ten years, two types of needs were addressed by two individuals who may have known nothing about each other. One was John Rex, a local plantation owner and tanner. The other was Dorothea Lynde Dix of Massachusetts, a guest at the Mansion House hotel on Fayetteville Street during the meeting of the General Assembly in 1848. Rex died in 1839. In his will he left some money for "the erection and endowment of an infirmary or hospital for the sick and afflicted poor of the city of Raleigh." Although more than fifty years passed before Rex Hospital opened as a charity hospital, the vision of one man had spurred the conscience and action of many. Miss Dix was in North Carolina to try to sway legislative help for the mentally ill. She became a friend of Cumberland County Representative

continued

The crowd-pleasers in this photograph, taken in 1898, are the circus elephants and entourage. The parade is proceeding west on Morgan Street and turning south onto Fayetteville Street, passing the Capitol, unseen beyond the trees in the upper left portion of the scene. The awninged structure was known as the Dortch Building. Although it is located on the Casso Tavern property, it is not the Casso building. The Dortch Building was built in the 1830s facing Fayetteville Street, replacing Peter Casso's which faced Morgan Street and which was destroyed in a June 1833 fire.

Preceding the Agriculture Building on this site was this continuously enlarged hotel, shown here next to the Labor Building. This 1903 photograph shows Edenton Street running in front of the buildings. The vacant street at the right of the photograph was Halifax Street, now closed to make Bicentennial Plaza. Continuously enlarged since the original portion was built in 1812 as the Eagle Hotel, the building became the Guion, and later the National Hotel. The state purchased it in 1881 and used it as the Agriculture Building, the first government office building outside Union Square.

James Dobbin and his wife, also guests in the hotel during the legislative session. When Mrs. Dobbin became ill, Miss Dix spent many hours providing care for her. Knowing that she was dying, she asked Miss Dix what she could do to repay her compassionate service to her. Miss Dix asked her to request her husband's support in the legislature for a facility in which to treat the mentally ill. Within a week the General Assembly had ratified the bill creating the State Hospital for the Insane in North Carolina, which opened in 1856 on a beautiful wooded hill in southwest Raleigh.

Many men and women chose deliberate roles in the course-making of Raleigh. One vital, enduring man chose an active course in Raleigh and lived to see most of his actions and influences take root in the first half-century. English-born newspaper editor Joseph Gales came to Raleigh where he continued his newspaper trade by creating the *Raleigh Register*. Although his was not the only newspaper in its time, nor his vibrant interest in the community an isolated case, Gales stands out as a daring pioneer, yet responsible citizen. Gales held many posts in the growing community. He was chosen to serve as a city commissioner in the municipal election in 1803. He served three terms as mayor of Raleigh, the last concluded with his death in 1841. Gales was part of the Neuse River Navigation Company, the short-lived experimental venture to send commerical cargoes between Wake County and the coast of North Carolina. From 1808 until he sold the last in 1833, Gales had a series of paper mills, which provided his newsprint, but not too much else. He investigated the extent of graphite mines near Raleigh, urged formation of a statewide mutual fire insurance company, and participated in the Agricultural Society of the State of North Carolina in 1818. Activities of the agricultural organization led eventually to a "Cattle Show and Exhibition of Domestic Manufactures and a Ploughing Match, to take place in Raleigh, in the month of October, annually," later known as the North Carolina State Fair. When Raleigh Academy opened on Burke Square in 1804, Gales was a trustee and secretary of the board of the academy, and later served as president. As Unitarians, Gales and his family knew something of the differing views of their Protestant neighbors, but earned respect as participants in activities of the Presbyterian Church and as colleagues of many ministers and laymen. Gales brought up at least two generations of newspapermen, gave vision to a railroad, and helped a toddling young city find sure footing.

And so it went in the early life of the capital town. The leaders, the experimenters, the builders, the observers, the tamers, found a place in a new frontier. In the middle of a newly-formed country, in the center of a southern state, the city of Raleigh, its people, that is, made their legacies for their natural and cultural descendants.

*The modern, sunlit chamber of
the House of Representatives is a
pleasant work place for its 120
members who, along with the
Senate, study and transform many
bills into state laws. Prior to 1961,
the House and Senate, the North
Carolina General Assembly, met
in rooms in the Capitol which are
also open to the public.*

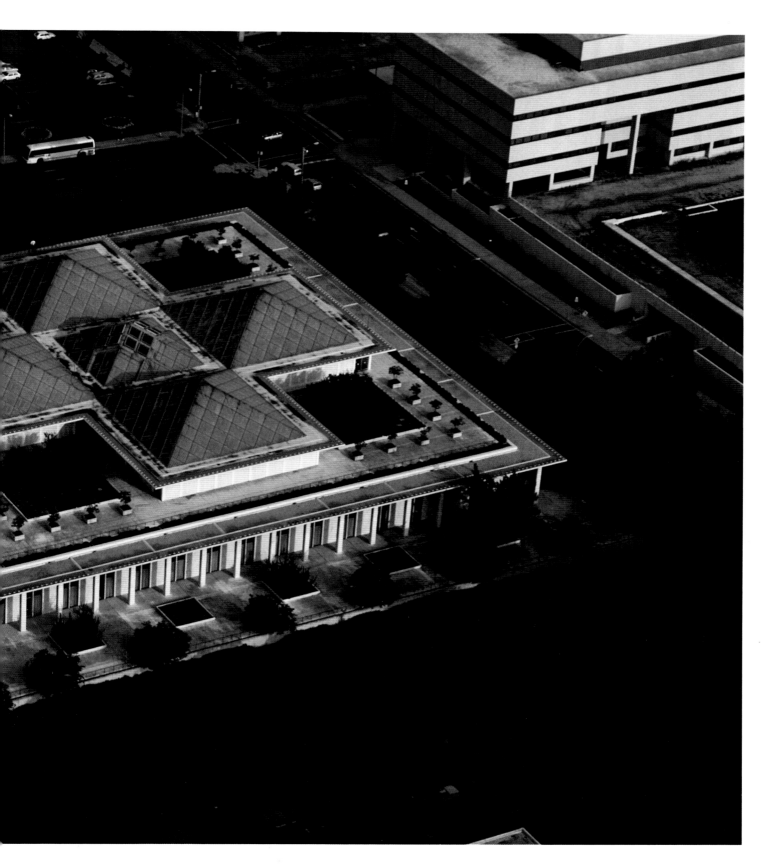

The distinctive architecture of the North Carolina State Legislative Building has elements of both classical and modern design. The work of Edward Durell Stone who also designed the John F. Kennedy Center for the Performing Arts in Washington, D.C., its foundation is a broad podium of North Carolina granite that measures 340 feet in width.

Each spring a ritual of healthy and energetic adventure occurs in the form of the Great Raleigh Road Race sponsored by Capitol Broadcasting Company, Inc. Some come to win; some come to finish. Often the humidity is the greatest competitor.

Raleigh drivers, the majority of whom are courteous and patient, choose the infamous beltline with its occasional delays over some other slower circuitous routes. For that routine trip to work and back, crowded though it is at peak times, the Cliff Benson Beltline has served well for many years. Its origins are in the "Master Transportation Plan" of 1946 and more specifically 1951, when a beltline highway was called for.

Along a corridor of trees, grazing horses are silhouetted against the purple and pink dusk at North Carolina State University's School of Veterinary Medicine. For the passerby the scene is restful and a reminder that not everything is brick and stone within the city boundaries. For the student who is progressing towards the Doctor of Veterinary Medicine degree in this fine four-year program, beauty is blended with

On Mimosa Street about ten blocks north of the Capitol, the Mordecai House offers an authentic look into the past. Built before 1785 and enlarged sometime prior to 1824, the restored house was part of a vast plantation where cotton, sweet potatoes, corn and other marketable commodities once provided sumptuous living for its owners.

Nature usually brings a respectable snowfall to Raleigh in January. On Adam Mountain in the north part of the city, the delicate, uncovered twigs and limbs were able to bear an inch or so of white weight during this particular storm.

It's Jazz in the Garden! On the site of the racetracks of the old fairgrounds the Raleigh Little Theatre Rose Garden is concert heaven. This is part of Artsplosure, the city's annual tribute to the visual and performing arts.

At Mordecai Historic Park, the first home of Andrew Johnson is one of a collection of original buildings, having been moved there in 1975. Besides the plantation manor house called Mordecai, the park contains the early nineteenth century double-door building, which was once a storehouse for the plantation; a smokehouse; a kitchen; and a recreated garden of the 1830s.

The tiny house in which President Johnson was born has travelled the city from its original site on Peter Casso's tavern property at the head of Fayetteville Street to East Cabarrus Street, then to Pullen Park, and finally to Mordecai Historic Park on Mimosa Street.

Although Andrew Johnson moved from Raleigh while still in his teens and returned on only a couple of occasions, it is fitting that the modest home of his birth, which escaped the disastrous Fayetteville Street fires of the 1830s and which was neglected for many years, has been preserved as part of the nation's history. Examples of family lifestyles of the early 1800s are displayed in the two-story house.

The miniature train, whose rumbling trek around Pullen Park delights youngsters, is but one feature of the 60-acre public property provided by R. Stanhope Pullen just over one hundred years ago. The C.P. Huntington Train Ride, a 1911 Dentzel Carousel, a kiddie boat ride, pedal boats, picnic shelters, and swimming pool complete this inner-city recreation area.

The variety of architectures found in Raleigh attests to the efforts of the valiant minority who strives to preserve remnants of past craftmanship and tradition amid the pressures of progress and modernization in the new era. The historical and preservation groups in Raleigh, in North Carolina, and, indeed, nationally, are to be commended.

Three men born in North Carolina became president of the United States. A bronze sculpture unveiled at Union Square by President Harry S. Truman honors Andrew Jackson, seventh President (1829-1837); James Knox Polk, eleventh President (1845-1849); and Andrew Johnson, seventeenth President (1865-1869).

A fine performance of Tchaikovsky's "The Nutcracker" was presented last Christmas season by the Raleigh School of Dance, the North Carolina School of the Arts, and the North Carolina Symphony.

World renowned violinist Itzhak Perlman performed in Reynolds Coliseum in 1983 and 1986 for Friends of the College. Since 1959 the local cultural organization has brought to North Carolina State University and to the city of Raleigh an outstanding assemblage of classical music and dance artists in a unique and highly successful manner. Students, at no charge at all, have attended over the years such performances as The London Symphony Orchestra with Andre Previn conducting, the National Ballet of Washington, pianist Andre Watts, and beloved operatic singer Beverly Sills. Friends of the College make it possible for the entire community to enjoy these programs at a price below that of an average movie ticket.

Interstate 40 supports much of the traffic between Raleigh, Durham, and the Research Triangle Park. From this unique vantage the remaining wooded areas of our civilization are beautifully visible.

Competitors pour it on in the men's 500-meter doubles in the kayaking event of the highly successful U.S. Olympic Festival in July, 1987. Canoeing, kayaking, and rowing, all fought out at Lake Wheeler south of Raleigh, were three of the thirty-four thrilling events conducted in Greensboro, Chapel Hill, Cary, Durham, Research Triangle Park, Kerr Lake, and Raleigh. Sponsored by North Carolina Amateur Sports, the two-week Olympic Festival was supported by dozens of businesses, hundreds of competitors and volunteers, and thousands of spectators.

A scene of solitude amid granite markers at one of Raleigh's cemeteries is a reminder that life on earth is temporal; so is a snowfall.

A carefully bricked walkway
maintains its deliberate
pattern after a light dusting
of January snow.

In a nearly colorless, furtive atmosphere six Revolutionary War heroes are larger-than-life in a twentieth-century American artist's oil canvas in the North Carolina Museum of Art on Blue Ridge Road in Raleigh.

From the classical period of art, the new headless form of Aphrodite of Cyrene occupies a sometimes sunny corner of the modern museum.

Traffic lights are meant for ordinary days. Occasionally a concert like Chuck Mangione's on the Capitol grounds draws an audience large enough to warrant the temporary closing of Morgan Street. It's all in a dayful of enjoyment when it's an Artsplosure event which is interrupting traffic.

*For an outdooor wedding one can scarcely improve on the sanctuary
provided by the WRAL-TV Gardens, an idyllic spot which also served as
studio-for-a-day for "CBS This Morning", one azalea-pretty day in April, 1988.*

*Two contemplative figures are a study in companionship, family sharing, or the
giving-learning cycle that is essential to human relationships. Here the older companion
is poised, framed in the act of passing to the other the legacy of any acquired fishing
skills. The two squat at water's edge at Umstead State Park, ten miles northwest of Raleigh.*

A look down Fayetteville Street by fireworks and laser light culminated festivities sponsored by the Raleigh Convention and Visitors Bureau that was a kick-off for Artsplosure in 1987. This view invites a comparison of older photographs taken at various vantage points which show the changing face of Raleigh's oldest street of commerce.

59

The North Carolina Symphony, one of the southeast's most excellent orchestras, performs approximately 400 adult and children's educational concerts each year in more than 100 communities across the state. It is a well-led, well-managed unit of excellence, and Conductor Gerhardt Zimmermann is largely credited for the calibre of guest artists.

The practiced wave of the baton by Assistant Conductor Jackson Parkhurst commands musical harmony on stage. In less formal attire, the North Carolina-trained conductor is coordinator, writer and producer of many Symphony extravaganzas, most often for children's groups.

The main entrance to the state Education Building, unusually angled, faces the corner of Salisbury and Edenton streets. Behind the rather intricate-patterned ironwork of one of the three identical front doors, an inside light penetrates the colorless glass creating a magical aura.

The sun-colored dome over the rotunda of the Capitol rises a stately 97½ feet from the base and forms a grand, if remote, canopy over the centerpiece figure, the 1970 copy of Antonio Canova's statue of George Washington.

The Capitol grounds, called Union Square, are a park-like collection of not only the impressive State House (as the original building was called), but more than a dozen widely-spaced statues and monuments which honor men and women and events from George Washington to the Vietnam War. Placed appropriately with them are weaponry and symbols such as this cannon of the Civil War era.

People are drawn to Union Square. It is a shady respite from the traffic and bustle of a weekday downtown; it is an open-air concert hall and rallying point on the weekend. On a day like this, though, the wrought-iron benches are lonely sculptures, abandoned by man, pigeon and squirrel.

The ten-day phenomenon known as Artsplosure, conducted for the ninth time in 1988, is meant to entertain and inspire children as well as adults. This young enthusiast tries her hand at mural painting.

Raleigh, the city of oaks. . . .No amount of technology can hurry the replacement of one lost tree.

Bikers of the harmless variety set out for a summer day of adventure. Neighborhood parks provided by civic groups, many dozens of major parks, and recreational lakes should offer enough for these two.

Men and women compete in The Old Reliable Run with the same vigor and for the same reasons as runners throughout the country; a chief motivation is the sheer pleasure of striving, enduring alongside either acquaintances or strangers who share that exhilaration. Groups such as the North Carolina Roadrunners Club also sponsor informal weekend runs at Shelley Lake and at Northridge Shopping Center.

In an age of fast, pre-prepared food, the word *fresh* is heard with less frequency, but spoken, perhaps, with more longing. However, *fresh* comes with the same requirements as in the days of taverns and inns: prepare soil, plant, cultivate, harvest, shell or strip, cook. Then eat.

Left to itself, the rapid-growing kudzu vine will dominate most any vacant lot and some infrequently-maintained yards.

A rider oversees a horse's snack time during the July Fourth Celebration at the State Fairgrounds.

Through the protective fence and summer foliage, the Executive Mansion of Burke Square is easily viewed. It has been the elaborate, distinctive official home of the North Carolina Governor since 1891. The Mansion is a prized example of Victorian architecture, a splendid arrangement of gables, balconies, spacious halls, and sixteen foot ceilings.

75

The labor of warmer seasons is appreciated in chillier days. These logs provide the fuel for heat which many Carolinians prefer to oil, gas or electric forms.

Although the sun has obscured the identification on the cars of this train, it is the necessary transportation of the Ringling Brothers and Barnum and Bailey Circus which stops at the State Fairgrounds for a week in February. During matinee and evening performances, nearby Dorton Arena is the Big Top for tumbling acts, clown antics, high wire talents and animal performances.

Delectable watermelons and canteloupes are
weekend fare at the Raleigh Farmers Market.
The outside stalls, frequented by Raleigh
shoppers in spring, summer and fall, may bear
some resemblance to Raleigh's old combination
City Hall and Market House which stood
between Exchange Street and Market Place. The
City Market at Moore Square, now redesigned,
was once the city produce center.

For a variety of fruits and vegetables, some
grown out-of-state, of course, it's the Raleigh
Famers Market, south of the beltline off
Downtown Boulevard. Besides the season's
edible abundance, one may shop for shrubs,
trees and flowering plants.

Where Wilmington and Salisbury Streets converge at
Peace Street, a tall structure dominates the terrain
and completes an ellipse that begins at the north end
of downtown Raleigh and ends just beyond South
Street at Memorial Auditorium at the point at which
Wilmington and Salisbury Streets meet again. The
Archdale Building, dramatic at night, houses the
Department of Natural Resources and Community
Development, Crime Control and Public Safety
offices, and is neighbor to the Dobbs Building in
which Department of Commerce offices are located.

Brilliant azaleas adorn Bicentennial Plaza near the
entrance to the Museum of Natural Sciences.

A restful stream reflects a sun-proud sky and thick trees, part of the charm of the Piedmont and repeated in and around the capitol city.

American Airlines came to Raleigh-Durham Airport in 1987 and in May, 1988, its Boeing 767 jetliner made a direct flight from RDU to Orly Airport in Paris, a first for North Carolina air travellers.

They make it look like fun. It is! During their seventeen years as a non-profit group, the Little German Band brings many of the polka-type dances and tunes of the Alpine to delighted audiences not only locally, but in states who observe Oktoberfest and Bavarian celebrations. The group was one of many at The International Festival in Raleigh in 1987, the Festival's second year.

What brings delight in adulthood is often sampled in formative years. The love for folk dances, as well as the appreciation for various cultures that usually accompanies the introduction of them, is both practical and entertaining in our multi-national society. Children and their informal audience enjoy the flavor of foreign nations on the Capitol grounds.

The tracks of the CSX railroad in night-glow color remind one of an industry as old as Raleigh itself. For a capital city far from navigable rivers, the comings and goings of people and goods by rail was for many years vital to growth and stability.

An overhead view from Boylan Street catches freight cars in off-duty hours. Although passenger rail service has been all but displaced by air and motor travel, the freight train is still in demand for transporting building materials, paper products, coal, and sometimes fruits and vegetables.

Very few events, modes of quiet transportation, or racing paraphernalia gain more spectators than hot-air balloon exhibitions. The Triangle Balloon Classic features an acrobatic air show, helicopter rides, live bands, and plenty of food and drink, but it is the airborne balloon, particularly dozens of them that act as pied piper for thousands of adults and children in sight of them on a certain humid weekend afternoon in August.

A multi-tentacled mushroom whirls about at the fairgrounds. Midway carnival rides provide much of the interest for young people at the North Carolina State Fair.

In the Microelectronics Laboratory of the Department of Electrical and Computer Engineering at North Carolina State University, researchers are involved in the fabrication of semiconductors.

A researcher in the NCSU Department of Materials Science and Engineering analyzes the composition of new materials with sophisticated probes in the Analytical Instrumentation Facility.

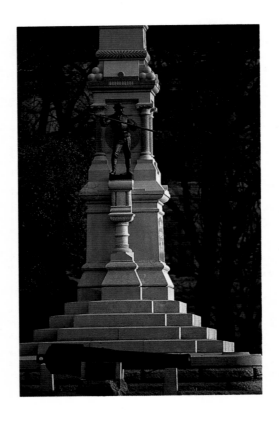

Placed well above eye level, but not nearly as high as another bronze soldier in the same piece, this representative war hero is part of a three-man Confederate Monument that dominates the west portion of Union Square. Representing infantry, cavalry, and artillery soldiers, the memorial was sponsored to honor the war dead from this state. Nearly one quarter of all Confederate casualties were North Carolinians. The condition of many of the monuments of Union Square has resulted from restoration work underwritten by the Women's Club of Raleigh, Inc., in this decade.

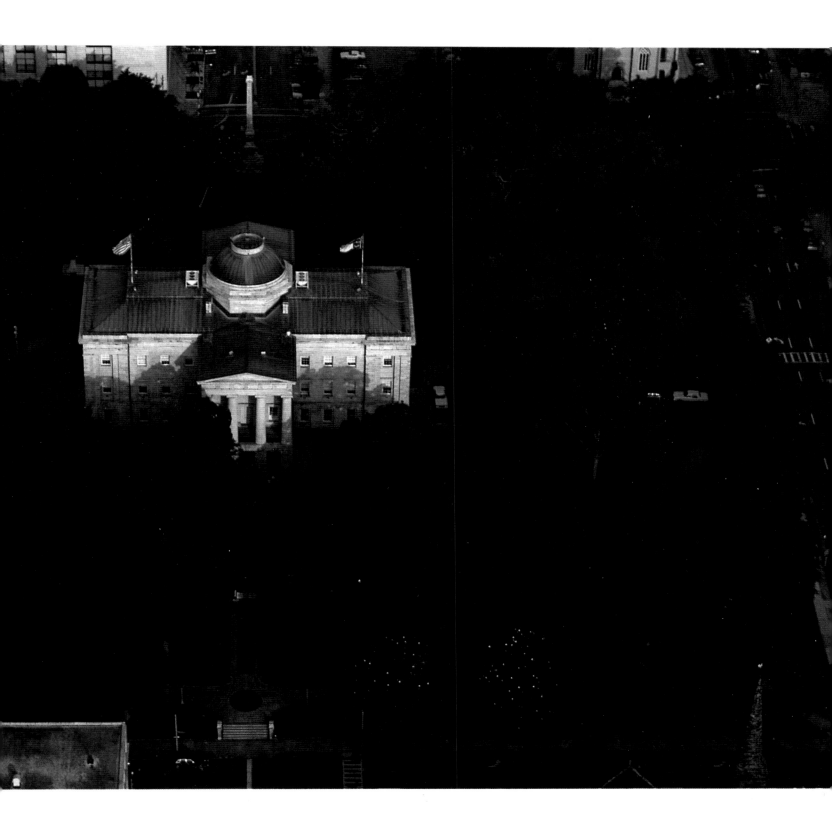

An aerial perspective of the Capitol reveals the east view, apparent because of the spire from historic Christ Church visible in the lower right corner. Once thick with young oak and hickory trees, Union Square was designed to be at the center of four wide thoroughfares which formed a cross shape in the 400-acre rectangle newly named Raleigh.

The marvelously constructed Dorton Arena, on the State Fairgrounds completed in 1952 and acclaimed by architects and critics for its new use of the old engineering principles of tension and compression, is parabolic in shape and as sound as anything that Hurricane Hazel tested back in 1954.

Applying two rules of athletic competition—concentration and consistent speed—are local entrants in the Watermelon Eating event, part of the all-day July Fourth Celebration at the State Fairgrounds.

This is no time to let up! Cyclists in a criterium race give heavy pedal performance in downtown Raleigh.

Training for cycling competition begins here. Or maybe this youngster simply likes the feel of the air brushing past him and the drive to the goal line, which is any spot he chooses.

To compare the buildings of First Baptist Church on Salisbury Street to those of Christ Episcopal Church nearby on Edenton Street, one might not expect to learn that both represent Gothic architecture. They do, although with variations. These oft-climbed steps represent a portion of historic First Baptist Church built in 1859.

As with many preserved structures in Raleigh, the Seaboard Office Building is not located on its original site, but sits on North Salisbury Street awaiting renovation, a bit of nineteenth century antiquity of painted brick with ornamental ironwork. Formally, the Raleigh + Gaston - Seaboard Coastline Building functioned as administrative offices for the railroad for more than 100 years.

In North Carolina nearly every adult and most children can be described as avid basketball fans. The true fanatics are a somewhat smaller group by comparison, but by no means invisible. You'll find them in friendly clusters at Reynolds Coliseum when North Carolina State University hosts ACC and non-conference foes. They have cause for confidence: in this decade alone they overpowered opponents when it counted most, and won two No. 1 spots in the ACC and a national championship title.

NC State athletics include a formidable showing of Wolfpack
football tactics at home games played in Carter-Finley
Stadium, and in games throughout the conference. The
university marching band is always proud to spell out
its allegiance to the 50,000 to 58,000 fans who line the
bleachers and grassy bank on the south end of the field at
nearly every game.

In an unrehearsed moment, a guitar player's music is easily matched in eloquence by the visual effect of autumn leaves reflected in the windows overhead. The stained-glass look in the Capitol's first floor windows supplies a warmth not usually associated with

In Oakwood Historic District, one finds this and two other homes built by James W. Lee for himself and for family members between 1872 and 1882. The homes have been referred to as "Steamboat Gothic" in architecture, yet the design is thought to be the work of architect William Percival, who also supplied the design for First Baptist Church.

The preservation of old homes in Raleigh is a respected, if expensive, endeavor. Oakwood was named Raleigh's first Historic District in 1975. Capitol Square and Blount Street are also official historic districts. The Raleigh Historic Sites Commission, appointed in 1961, and supportive groups of the Commission have encouraged many restorations in the city.

Playing to a full house were the competitors in the diving events of the U.S. Olympic Festival held at Candler Swim Club, during which Greg Louganis out-performed all contenders.

Opening and closing ceremonies for the Festival, extraordinary evenings for North Carolinians, were held at Carter-Finley Stadium in Raleigh. Some 52,700 spectators joined national champions, military bands, torch runners, and Mercury astronauts for the sensational programs.

The orange-rust of fall is repeated in the vivid oak leaves overhead. From the oft-spoken comments one hears each year, the beauty of multi-colored, though dying leaves, still hanging, never gets monotonous.

An array of pumpkins at a roadside stand is an autumn tradition that doesn't change much from year to year. But it's something like shopping for Christmas trees: they aren't all quite the same. You like to pick out the one you want.

Two wind surfers command their crafts on one of the Raleigh area's recreational lakes. In rhythm with the lilt and lap of the gentle surface, the pair can maneuver at close proximity for a long ride. Accessible lakes like Jordan, Falls and Wheeler offer enough acres for most any water sports.

Two proud flags flank a configuration of two modern buildings, the Legislative and the Archdale. In a shot that gives the effect of compressing space, it doesn't seem possible that 1,270 feet separate the two governmental buildings.

Proud, august Memorial Auditorium was built at the foot of Fayetteville Street, although the Civic Auditorium complex interrupts a clear path up the street to the Capitol. On the same site Municipal Auditorium had been build in the early years of the twentieth century. It burned, perhaps because of carelessness, in 1830. Prior to the days of an auditorium, the Governor's "Palace" occupied the lot. The new Memorial Auditorium was dedicated to the war dead of Raleigh, and since 1932, has seen governor's inaugurations, debutantes balls, concerts, and theatrical performances. It is the home of the North Carolina Symphony.

The firm foundation of Wake County granite supports homes and businesses and the Capitol Building at Union Square. Here at 115 West Morgan Street the famous Raleigh Water Tower remains, and with impunity. It is thirty feet of granite, brought from Rolesville Quarry, and laid octagonally, three feet thick with fifty-five feet of hand-made bricks in the same configuration continuing to the top. In 1963, the Raleigh Historic Sites Commission effected enduring status for the 101-year-old tower, although the huge wooden water tank on top has not been preserved.

The Court of Appeals building on Morgan Street opposite the Capitol is the earliest of the state's twentieth century buildings, a grand granite edifice that originally held the Supreme Court and State Library and later known as the Ruffin Building.

The International Festival was spawned by a project of the Sister Cities in which Raleighites were encouraged to form groups which together would recognize, creatively and actively, various countries and cultures. From the first festival in 1986 an annual program has emerged, and it doesn't look as if the end of its popularity is in sight.

It's not the shade of an old oak tree, but a stretch in a hammock carefully secured in a truck that hauled watermelons and cantaloupes to the Farmers Market is a cool, temporary time-out.

For the Raleighite who likes a little country mixed with his urban lifestyle, this pastoral scene awaits travellers on Hillsborough Street daily. It is part of State's School of Veterinary Medicine, but for the driver devoid of medical vision the restful view can be very pleasurable.

A regal tower looms above a green corner on Hillsborough Street. It is Memorial Tower, North Carolina State University's handsome structure which bears a clock on each of its four sides and a Shrine Room to commemorate the school's World War I dead.

A dynamic sample of Islamic-influenced art is the large bright canvas by American-born Frank Stella, a permanent work at the North Carolina Museum of Art.

In a look back to the Late Period of Egyptian art, one finds an example of a female mummy case carved from wood and lastingly painted.

This converted step-saver is not nearly as versatile as a skateboard and will probably soon be transporting baggage and boxes again from automobiles to East Building or Ross Residence Hall on Peace College campus. In the meantime, two students are game for a two-or-three mile-an-hour joy ride. Each of the three girls' colleges in Raleigh was established in the nineteenth century. St. Mary's, then Peace, and finally Meredith, which will soon be noting its 100th anniversary, all contribute a solid educational foundation for the workplace or for further studies.

At sundown a monochrome shimmer and a lone sailor form the stage and the set for an extravagant performance of color and shadow.

The open, unprotected doorway to this house suggests that it is being relocated. Some of Raleigh's older houses and offices are moved to protected sites when they have not been converted into functional facilities, but may be scheduled for refurbishing as worthy examples of bygone styles of living. As with any true work of art, the story related in this simple scene is not easily uncovered, but has merit of its own.

*For more than two years venerable
Moore Square has served as outdoor
gallery to a unique sculpture, a 10-foot
high by 24-foot long piece entitled "The
Wilderness Screen."*

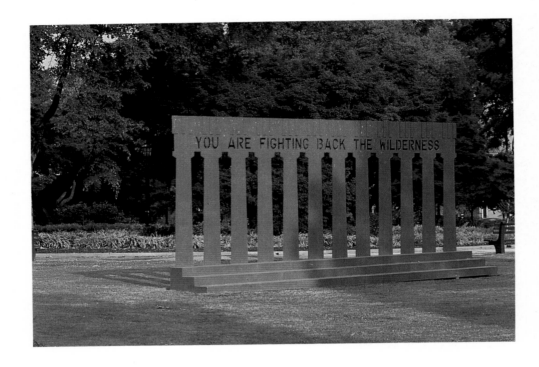

In the older neighborhoods, as at 400 Polk Street in Oakwood Historic District, a gesture of patriotism comes quite easily.

North Carolina native and nationally-acclaimed songstress Roberta Flack wowed the crowd at Carter-Finley Stadium in Olympic Festival Opening Ceremonies. For Miss Flack, fresh from her participation in the July Fourth festivities at the U.S. Capitol in Washington, D.C., her appearance in Raleigh was combined with a reunion with relatives from her Black Mountain girlhood home.

Raleigh Area Historical Organizations

Badger-Iredell Law Office Foundation
Colonial Dames of America
Historic Preservation Foundation of
  North Carolina
Mordecai Historic Park
Mordecai Square
Raleigh Historic District Commission
Raleigh Historic Properties Commission
Society for the Preservation of
  Historic Oakwood
State of North Carolina Preservation
  Office
Wake County Historical Society

Raleigh Area Arts Agencies

Arts Access, Inc.
Arts Together
Artspace, Inc.
Artsplosure
Ballet Theatre Company
Capital Area Arts Foundation
Capital Area Community Chorus
Capital City Dance Company
Cinema, Inc.
City Gallery of Contemporary Art
City of Raleigh Arts Commission
Concert Dancers
Dance Project
Dance Associates of Raleigh
Estey Hall Foundation
National Opera Company
North Carolina Bach Festival
North Carolina Symphony
North Carolina Theatre
People for the Arts
Pinecone
Preservation Jazz Company, Inc.
Rainbow Company
Raleigh Boychoir
Raleigh Chamber Music Guild
Raleigh Civic Ballet
Raleigh Concert Band
Raleigh Consort
Raleigh Dance Theatre
Raleigh Ensemble Players
Raleigh Fine Arts Society
Raleigh Little Theatre
Raleigh Oratorio Society
Raleigh Photographic Arts Association
Raleigh Symphony Orchestra
Raleigh-Wake Symphony Orchestra
  Development Association, Inc.
St. Augustine Community Theatre
Theatre in the Park
Wake Visual Arts Association
Wake County Arts Council
WCPE Radio

The designer's details and creative influence on the old Capitol Building were carried through on each floor. The curve of the worn staircase, with its patterned ironwork is part of the charm and ambiance of the state's most distinguished government building. Art and architecture endure, and the heart of Raleigh does not move north, but lingers around Union Square.